DADDY'S PROMISE

"Reunited by Love: A Daughter's Journey"

Written By

Taron Hill

Inspired by a True Event

About the Author

My name is Taron Hill. At the age of 18, I was charged, convicted, and sentenced to 60 years in prison for a crime I did not commit. After suffering, begging, and pleading for 16 1/2 years, I was ultimately exonerated and reunited with my daughter. For more information on my story, please Google "Taron Hill of New Jersey." You can also catch my documentary on WETV, "Innocent After Lockup," Episode Taron.

It is my sincere hope that this book will provoke empathy, ignite a passion for justice, and spark a meaningful dialogue about the importance of safeguarding the rights and dignity of all individuals within our legal system.

Special thanks to my daughter Niya who inspired this story, and to all the courageous individuals who have faced similar challenges with unwavering courage and grace.

May this book serve as a beacon of hope, raising awareness and understanding of the profound impact of wrongful convictions on families and communities worldwide.

Together, let us strive for a world where justice is truly blind and where the voices of the wrongfully convicted are heard and honored. This book is for you.

ABOUT THE BOOK

A young girl named Niya's heart beat with the rhythm of hope and longing. From the moment she entered the world, she yearned to be held in the embrace of her father, Mr. Hill, a man who had been wrongfully convicted when she was just a newborn. As Niya grew into a determined and resilient young girl, her father's absence left a permanent mark on her heart. However, amidst the pain, a flicker of hope remained, a hope that one day, her father would return home.

This is the story of Niya's unwavering faith, her father's enduring promise, and the remarkable journey that led to their long-awaited reunion. It is a tale of resilience, love, and the unbreakable bond between a father and his daughter.

Join Niya as she embarks on a heartfelt journey, seeking the light of hope in the darkness and discovering the extraordinary power of love to overcome all obstacles. Through the pages of this book, let us explore the heartwarming tale of "Reunited by Love: A Daughter's

Journey" and witness the remarkable bond that transcends time and distance.

TABLE OF CONTENT

DADDY'S PROMISE

In a small town surrounded by rolling hills and blooming meadows, there lived a bright and spirited girl named Niya. Niya had a heart as courageous as a lion and a smile that could light up even the darkest days. But in the midst of her joy, there was a lingering sadness. Her father, Mr. Hill, had been taken away when she was just a newborn, wrongfully convicted of a crime he didn't commit.

Niya's mother often told her stories about her father's kindness and love for his family. She showed Niya the letters he sent, each one filled with promises to come back home and be with them once again. Niya cherished those letters, holding onto the hope of a reunion with her father.

As the years passed, Niya grew into a determined and resilient young girl. She discovered a love for painting and spent hours capturing the beauty of the world on her canvas. But beneath her artistic spirit, a longing for her father's presence never faded. She often found herself gazing at the stars, wondering if he was looking at the same sky.

On the day of Niya's sixteenth birthday, her mother gathered the family and said, "I have something important to share with you, my dear Niya. After years of hard work and dedication, a team of lawyers and kind-hearted people have proven your father's innocence. He's coming back home to us!"

Niya's heart swelled with joy and disbelief. The news felt like a dream she was afraid to wake up from. She thought of all the times she had yearned for her father's embrace and imagined the stories he would tell her when he returned.

As the days passed, Niya's anticipation grew stronger. She spent hours preparing for her father's return, painting vibrant murals on the walls of her room, and organizing a welcoming celebration with her family and friends. The house buzzed with excitement, and Niya's heart beat with the rhythm of hope.

Finally, the long-awaited day arrived. Niya stood at the front door, her hands trembling with anticipation, as a car pulled up to the house. With each approaching step, the sound of her heart grew louder until the door swung open, revealing a figure she had only known through letters and faded photographs.

"Daddy!" Niya exclaimed, her eyes filled with tears of joy. Her father stood before her, a hint of disbelief in his eyes as he gazed at the young woman his little girl had become. Without a word, they embraced, holding onto each other as if they were making up for the lost years.

In the days that followed, Niya and her father savored every moment together. They shared stories, laughter, and quiet moments of understanding. Niya learned about her father's unwavering faith and how he had held onto hope through the darkest times.

As they sat and watched the sunset one evening, Niya asked her father, "How did you keep your promise to us for all those years when you were so far away?"

Her father smiled; his eyes mirrored the glimmering stars and began to tell her a story.

"When I was taken away from you and your mom, I made a promise to myself that no matter how far apart we were, I would always be there for you in spirit," her father said. "I knew that one day the truth would come to light, and I held onto that hope with all my heart."

"I spent my time in prison writing letters, imagining the day we would be reunited. I wanted you to know that you were never alone and that I loved you more than anything in the world," he continued. "Every birthday, every holiday, and every ordinary day, I held onto the hope of coming back to you."

Niya listened with great attention, feeling a rush of emotions as she realized the depth of her father's love and determination. "You never gave up, even when things seemed impossible," she whispered, her eyes shimmering with admiration.

"Never, my dear Niya. I made a promise to you and your mom, and I was determined to keep it," her father said, his voice filled with warmth.

As the days turned into weeks, Niya and her father shared many special moments. They went for walks in the park, cooked meals together, and even worked on a painting that captured the essence of their reunion. Niya cherished each and every day, savoring the simple joys of having her father by her side.

One sunny afternoon, Niya's father took her to a quiet spot beneath a towering oak tree. They sat together, the gentle rustle of leaves providing a soothing backdrop to their conversation.

"Niya, I want you to know that even though I missed so many years of your life, you were always in my thoughts and in my heart," her father said, his eyes filled with emotion. "I may have missed your first steps and your childhood adventures, but I will always be here for you now."

Niya felt a rush of love and understanding wash over her. She realized that while her father may have missed many milestones, their bond was unbreakable, and their love was timeless.

Together, they made a pact to create new memories and cherish the moments they had been given. They laughed, shared dreams, and embraced the simple beauty of being together as a family.

As time went on, Niya's father became a fundamental aspect of her life, offering guidance, encouragement, and unwavering support. They worked on art projects together, explored new hobbies, and celebrated the everyday wonders of life.

Niya's father filled their home with stories of resilience, hope, and the enduring power of love. He taught her to see the world through a lens of compassion and understanding, and Niya blossomed under his gentle guidance.

Years passed, and Niya grew into a confident and compassionate young woman, carrying her father's wisdom and love in her heart. She pursued her dreams with determination and grace, knowing that her father's unwavering support would always be with her.

One evening, as Niya and her father sat beneath the starlit sky, she whispered, "Thank you, Daddy, for never giving up and for keeping your promise. You've shown me the true meaning of strength and love."

Her father smiled, his eyes reflecting the shimmering stars above. "My dear Niya, you have always been my source of strength and taught me the true meaning of resilience and hope. I am so proud of the remarkable young woman you have become," he said, his voice filled with pride and love.

As they sat together, enjoying the calm of the peaceful night, Niya and her father knew that their bond was unbreakable. They had overcome the greatest of challenges, and their love had endured through the passage of time.

From that day forward, Niya and her father continued to create beautiful memories, embracing each day with gratitude and joy. Their story became a testament to the enduring power of love, hope, and the unbreakable bond between a father and his daughter.

THE END.

<u>*AWARENESS*</u>

There are 2.3 million individuals currently locked up in the United States of America. Studies show that between 4% - 6% of those individuals are actually innocent. Some studies even suggest that those numbers may be even higher. That's roughly around 115,000 innocent men and women sitting behind bars for something they didn't do.

HERE ARE SOME OF THE MOST COMMON CAUSES THAT LEAD TO A WRONGFUL CONVICTION!

1. Mistaken Witness Identification - Leading cause! (Eyewitness misidentifications are known to have played a role in 70% of the 349 wrongful convictions that were overturned based on DNA evidence)

2. False Confession - (Yes, it's true, innocent men & women actually have admitted to crimes they didn't commit. Most of these situations come from bad police practices)

3. False Forensic Evidence - (Where police or some form of government official plants or creates false evidence in order to secure a conviction)

4. Perjury - (A police or some form of government official testifies under oath and lies)

5. Official Misconduct - (Some form of government official does something wrong throughout the course of the investigation)

WHAT ARE YOUR MIRANDA RIGHTS?

1. You have the right to remain silent.

2. Anything you say can and will be used against you in a court of law.

3. You have the right to an attorney.

4. If you cannot afford an attorney, one will be provided for you.

5. Do you understand the rights I've just read to you? With these rights in mind, do you wish to speak to me?